Angels, Love and Light

By

John T. Goltz

White Fire Publishing

Angels, Love and Light

By John T. Goltz

Copyright © 2010 John T. Goltz

Published by:
White Fire Publishing
Tampa, Florida
www.whitefirepublishing.com

Cover Art: John T. Goltz

All rights reserved. This book may not be reproduced in whole or in part, without written permission from the publisher, except by a reviewer who may quote brief passages in a review; nor may any part of this book be reproduced, stored in a retrieval system, or transmitted in any form or by any other means electronic, mechanical, photocopying, recording, or other, without written permission from the publisher.

Library of Congress Control Number: 2010929594

ISBN: 978-0-979046-04-9

First Printing: June 2010
Printed in the USA on acid free paper

Foreword

On rare occasions, we are afforded the opportunity to experience inspiration that touches the depths of our souls. Such moments are gifts that delight the very core of our being and encourage us to expand our awareness beyond the norm.

These poems are filled with treasures that tickle our imagination and remind us of our true heritage as divine beings of light. John calls us back to the memory of our angelic self as we explore the joy of a loving moment.

This talented author provides the ingredients and all we add is our openness to enjoy a delightful feast of the heart.

Harold W. Becker
Author, *Unconditional Love - An Unlimited Way of Being*

Angels, Love and Light

Angels, Love and Light

Taking Flight
To My Beloved
Angels All Around
To Know Thyself
Hello Angels, Are You There?
Music To Dance With
Patience
Our True Nature
The Graceful Willow
Angels, Love and Light
Courage
Freedom
I Am
Dawn of a New Day
Being Me
Senses
Let Go
Sunrise
To Be An Angel
Grace
I Smile Inside
Temple In My Heart
The Beauty of My Soul
Thank You
The Magic Breath
The Gift of Light
Angel Visit
The Angel Peace
The Great Being

Calling All Angels
I Believe In You
Facing Fear
Conscious Acts of Kindness
You Are A Star
Separation
Heaven is Where the Heart Is
Relationships
Children
The Gift
The Angel of Gold
Sailing Home
New World

Angels, Love and Light

Angels,

Love

and

Light

Angels, Love and Light

Taking Flight

Like caterpillars evolving
               into beautiful butterflies

We humans are magnificent
        divine
               angelic beings

It is time that we recognize
            our true inner nature

               spread our wings

                   and fly.

Angels, Love and Light

To My Beloved

Lovely to behold
is the one that's true of heart
For with that inner radiance
there is wisdom to impart

It is beauty that transcends all form
and comes from deep within
It has been spoken of for ages past
for it is how we all begin

And lovely too are eyes that sparkle
with the love that beauty makes
Eyes will tell the truthful tale
of love that can't be faked

A life that is lived with harmony
allows the light to flow
And along the banks of the river light
it is beauty that does grow

Lovely to behold
is the open, radiant heart
It is you that I am speaking of
and the beauty you impart.

Angels, Love and Light

Angels All Around

There are angels all around us
    that shower us with love

They fill our lives with beauty
    and gifts from up above

There are angels for protection
    and angels just for fun

There are even mighty cosmic angels
    from out the central sun

Angels help our lives to flow
    even though we may resist

So why not let them do their job
    and allow them to assist.

Angels, Love and Light

To Know Thyself

To know thyself
        is a great admonition
Not a fanciful thing,
        but a true proposition

So what does it mean
        and where to begin
Perhaps to forgive
        and let go of sin

But sin is not judgment
        from heaven above
It is being untrue to yourself
        when your heart speaks of love

So be yourself
        and to your own heart be true
And peace you will find
        in just being you.

Hello Angels, Are You There?

Hello angels,
      are you there?

Of course we are,
      oh dearest one,
            we never travel far

Then tell me of some magic thing
      or a story from afar

We love to tell of marvelous things
      of which you will delight
For we never tell of scary things
      or things that might give fright

Perhaps you'd like to hear
      of the temple made of gold
Or the cutest little angel fairies
      who really are quite bold

There are marvels in this earth alone
      that could fill up many books
And good will always show itself
      if for good is what you look

We also know the special place
        where the greater part of you exists
It is sparkling white and super bright
        and of light it does consist

We would love to show you pictures
        and share a great deal more
If it is truth that you are seeking
        then there is much for you in store

So just keep on asking questions
        and the truth shall be revealed
Your heart will be your truest guide
        and will tell you what is real.

Angels, Love and Light

Music To Dance With

The music of heaven dances in my soul

It yearns to express
        to sing
                to dance
                        to go with the flow

I hear it speaking to me
        if I could only
                let go

I feel a tingle
        a smile
                and lo and behold

I dance
        with the music
                I express my soul.

Patience

Patience is a virtue
    or so the saying goes
But what exactly is it
    and who would really know

I think it means to put aside
    the noisy mental chatter
And focus on the joy in life
    and things that truly matter

Patience means to wait a moment
    and let the light appear
For in that light all is resolved
    and all things are made clear

Angels know what patience means
    and possess it all the time
They are with us when we need them
    and even when we're fine

Perhaps it is time that trips us up
      when searching for an answer
Patience means in perfect time
      just like a graceful dancer

Yes patience is a virtue
      I know it to be true
Its honor and nobility
      are all things found in you.

Angels, Love and Light

Our True Nature

Flowers burst into radiant splendor
    that we may surround ourselves
        with beauty

Birds sing the sweet songs of the seasons
    that we may be reminded of
        the music of the spheres

And the sun shines
    it's ever present gift of life
        that we may know
            our true nature.

Angels, Love and Light

The Graceful Willow

I sit quietly beneath a willow tree
    and marvel at its beauty and grace

It bows and waves to me in acknowledgement
    then goes on
        dancing with the wind

I have never thought the willow
    to be a sad tree
        for it is far too playful

And I have never seen a willow weep
    yet I have seen a willow
        overflow with love

It is angelic in a way
    with wings to enfold and comfort,
    a limb to lean on, a branch to dance with
    and a friend to talk to that never judges

As I sit quietly with my friend, the willow,
    our hearts sing a duet
        and dance
            as one
                with the wind.

Angels, Love and Light

Angels, Love and Light

I like to think of angels
    and love and light and peace
For to focus on these higher things
    allows their gifts to now release

To focus on my angel friends
    brings light into my heart
Then I overflow with love
    and joy I do impart

Humanity is in great need
    of the peace that angels bring
We can help our angel messengers
    if love and joy is what we sing

So focus on the higher realms
    and let your feelings take to flight
And when you look inside your heart
    You will find angels, love and light.

Courage

If you ask someone what courage means
      they will tell you many things
I think it means to face yourself
      despite the pain it seems to bring

There are many things that people do
      that are simple and routine
And there are many things that people dread
      and you know of what I mean

One may find it easy
      to take on monumental tasks
While to forgive or to say thank you
      is far too much to ask

There are others who are quite polite
      and a delight to be around
Yet in their inner worlds are fears
      that keep them rather bound

It takes courage and strength beyond belief
        to face your inner fears
Yet the rewards are great to learn from life
        and have your thoughts and feelings clear

So call upon your angel friends
        and muster up your will
Find the courage to expand your world
        and all good things you will fulfill.

Freedom

Freedom is our watch word

Freedom is our goal

It takes courage
               strength
                           and patience

To know the essence of our soul.

Angels, Love and Light

I Am

I am free
    like an angel
        and take on many forms

I laugh and I listen
    I am never far away
        I am never gone at all

I am a friend
    a good book
        or a pink and golden sunset

I am a mothers touch
    and a fathers
        helping hand

You know me
    because
        I am you

You are me
    through
        and through

I am unconditional love
    and you
        are too!

Angels, Love and Light

Dawn of a New Day

Like the sun blessing the earth
    with the rays of a new day

We, too, can bless our fellow man
    with the gift of forgiveness

And with this gift, all life shall receive
    the joy of a new beginning

And the chance for love
    to dawn once more
        upon the face of man.

Angels, Love and Light

Being Me

I am a spiritual being
    having a human experience

I follow my heart
    I seek and experience joy

I release all rules and roles
    that no longer feel good

I am my own role model
    and my own best friend

I embrace change
    and find comfort in knowing
    I do not have to stay the same

I can be anything I want to be
    That is part of the guarantee

I feel the best when
    I am just being me.

Senses

Touch the flame
    the spark of life

Feel the heartbeat
    pulse with light

See the beauty
    let joy take flight

Taste the freedom
    that is yours by right

Hear the music
    the spheres of might

Know the power
    of love and light

Sense the splendor
    ascend to great heights.

Angels, Love and Light

Let Go

Let go dear one
    let go

Allow life to flow
    and let go

There is no need to worry, fret or fear
    that is why I am here

There is a higher part of you
    that magically appears

In friends and family
    to dry up all the tears

Let life do what it does best
    get out of the way
    stop controlling
    start enjoying
    allow perfection to manifest

Trust dear one
    and let go.

Angels, Love and Light

Sunrise

As the sun rises and
        paints the sky

I feel the eternity of my soul
        knocking at the door of my heart

I gently close my eyes with the bright
        rays of light
        and turn my attention within

The sun rises also in me
        and lights my mind
        and fills my soul
        until I know myself as light

A being of light I am

A dazzling angel
        one with the great central sun

There is no more separation
        I am one with all life

As the sun eternally rises in my heart
        it paints my life
        with the colors of joy.

Angels, Love and Light

To Be An Angel

I want to be an angel
    to share messages of love

I want to be an angel
    to fly and laugh and be free

I want to be an angel
    to radiate joy, peace and harmony

I want to be an angel
    to serve and help and be

I am an angel now
    if that is what I choose to be.

Angels, Love and Light

Grace

Sunlight catches the mist of a waterfall

Glitter dances
    in celebration of the new year

A diamond embraced by silver
    blesses the union of two souls

An angel leaves a trail of radiant smiles

And Grace is always there
    on silver wings
        blessing all

With the wish to let go
    have fun
        love
        and enjoy the moment.

I Smile Inside

Flowers dance with morning dew

The sun smiles and says, "I Love You!"

With no conditions, limits or judgments

I smile inside

    look to the sky

        and beam

"I love me too!"

Angels, Love and Light

Temple In My Heart

There is a temple in my heart
      that is filled with light and love

It is the anchor point of light
      from heaven up above

I can see it in my mind
      in all its glorious splendor

And I feel its warmth and grandeur
      as it pours forth all its treasure.

Angels, Love and Light

The Beauty of My Soul

My eyes lock eyes with my eyes
as I gaze into the mirror of my soul

There is great beauty there
a friend, a good person, a kind and loving soul

I hear my own words of wisdom
that I deserve all the good that life offers

So I give myself permission to receive
and give to life the gift of receiving

And I complete the cycle by choosing
to live a life filled with peace and joy and ease

I nurture myself, I honor myself, I love myself
as I reflect upon the beauty of my soul.

Angels, Love and Light

Thank You

Thank you for the sunshine
    and thank you for the rain

Thank you for the gentle breeze
    the mountains and the plains

Thank you for the gift of life
    I am grateful that I'm here

And thank you for a heart that beats
    to remind me that you're near.

Angels, Love and Light

The Magic Breath

Take a deep breath
        and what do you feel
A wondrous strength
        and magic that's real

"Magic?" you say,
        "In a breath? Oh, please"
I assure you it is true
        just try it and see

Breath contains power
        to calm and to heal
It is pure life essence
        when you are quiet you can feel

It is an inside-out hug
        bringing comfort and love
Whenever we need help
        from heaven above

So take a deep breath
        and you will find that it's true
That breathing is magic
        it will make you feel new.

The Gift of Light

Like the sun blessing the earth
                    with the gift of light

So, too, do angels shine their rays
                    to fill our souls

That we may give the gift
                    of love and light

To all upon this planet
                    we call home.

Angel Visit

A visit from an angel
      is a blessed thing indeed
For angels don't take kindly
      to anger, lust or greed

Angels love to play
      and are attracted to your joy
You will find them very near you
      if it is love that you employ

Angels also comfort
      and lend a helping hand
Whenever we need special help
      or call assistance to our stand

Some have seen their angels
      when their life is in extreme
There are wiser ways to see them
      and more joyful I would deem

If you want to know your angels
    then maintain harmony inside
And let go the outer senses
    for within us they reside

You may ask for them to show themselves
    then pay attention to the signs
Angels act in subtle ways
    which are always quite divine

So train yourself to be
    in a state of listening grace
And angels will often visit
    and greet you face to face.

Angels, Love and Light

The Angel Peace

There is a mighty angel
      who is known to us as Peace
He guards us and protects us
      from our strife he does release

Peace pours to us his mighty rays
      containing light and love
When we open to receive the light
      we feel the peaceful dove

Peace is like the sunshine
      that we find within us all
And even when a storm appears
      it is Peace that heeds our call

Peace may be a feeling
      and a thought that all is well
Yet Peace is more a way to live
      that only living it can tell

You will find that Peace lives in you
      and will show you what to do
If it is Peace that you desire
      then to Peace you must be true.

The Great Being

I am a great being
    of light and love
Wwith you this moment
    bearing gifts from above

So open your heart
    and let your mind expand
And soon you will know
    and truly understand

It is I who is with you
    every moment of life
For I am an angel
    to keep you from strife

I can fill you with courage
    or strength as need be
If only you will let me
    it is then that you'll see

So turn your attention
> to the light in your heart
And sense the vibrations
> for you will find they are smart

Your heart has the wisdom
> to know what to do
And all that you need
> will come from there too

Always know I am with you
> and as bright as the sun
And know you're a great being
> because we are one.

Calling All Angels

Angels and guides
      great beings of light
Play with me, be with me
      hear me tonight

Talk with me, speak with me
      fill me with light
I know that you hear me
      now come into sight

I want to be with you
      to help and to serve
I know that through service
      it is then that I learn

Fill me with wisdom
      love, light and peace
I will do my part
      to help earn my keep

I will maintain my harmony
        and balance my mind
I know I am an angel
        and will do things in kind

To help one another
        is part of the fun
And know the good feeling
        the "Law of One"

I know you are here
        with me lighting the way
Thank you for coming
        I trust that you'll stay.

I Believe In You

I am a cosmic angel
to help you with your plight
So give up all your struggle
and stop the inner fight

You know you have great talent
and a heart of gold that's true
Now find your strength that is deep inside
the part I know as you

The world awaits your precious gifts
that only you can give
And acting in this manner
is what it means to live

But rather than get busy
and wonder what to do
I urge you to get quiet
to find what's right for you

Your heart contains the wisdom
and the part you are to play
But you must be in the moment
or your thoughts may try to sway

Do not listen to suggestions
and patterns based on fear
Turn your attention inward
and know that I am near

You have got a destiny
and plan to be fulfilled
You will know it when you do it
because your feelings will be thrilled

Just trust yourself, and know yourself
and believe in who you are
So no matter what the task you do
you will know that you are a star.

Angels, Love and Light

Facing Fear

Lessons that I thought were learned
    keep coming back to haunt
There must be something more to learn
    or these issues would not taunt

Perhaps it is like a spiral,
    ever upward do I go
I am stronger and I am wiser,
    it is doubt that blocks the flow

I know that I am capable
    or I would not be here now
I will show these problems who's in charge
    and before me they will bow

I call upon my angel friends
    and find my strength within
But first I find the love inside
    the best place to begin

These problems will resolve themselves
    and new ones may appear
Yet I know that I am master
    and triumphant over fear.

Angels, Love and Light

Conscious Acts of Kindness

Like the gentle breeze
    rustling the leaves on a tree
Angels make themselves known
    if we but raise our attention to notice

Yet like the wind
    it is the effect they leave behind
        that we recognize
And the good feeling in our heart
    that confirms the source of joy

Perhaps we have all had angels in our midst
    but only saw them
        for their thoughtful gifts

And perhaps we have been known as well
    for special things
        simply done, not said

For I believe there are angels all around us
    and a soulful search
        will expose this truth

We are all but angels in human clothes
    and reveal ourselves
        through our conscious
            acts of kindness.

Angels, Love and Light

You Are A Star

You are more than who you think you are
    of this I am quite sure
I know you as a shining star
    with a heart that's always pure

Your outer personality
    may be limited in scope
I am here to tell you honestly
    that we angels have great hope

So shed your layers, let go the fear
    and you will see the light
And as your thoughts begin to clear
    you may see with inner sight

You are the noblest of angels
    that has forgotten your great might
You are a star upon this earthly home
    and it is time to share your light.

Angels, Love and Light

Separation

Separation is a game we've played
    that has gone on for far too long
It may have had its challenges
    yet resistance makes us strong

The game is up, it is over
    we can call it now complete
We can give up pride and ego
    and the urge that says compete

It is time to take responsibility
    and create with conscious choice
To be honest and harmonious
    and deceit we will not foist

To be separate from the source of life
    is a thing that can't be done
For life is in us and around us
    it is called the "Law of One"

So stop this silly nonsense
    that says that you're alone
And know that love is in you
    and the Universe your home.

Heaven is Where the Heart Is

Heaven is where the heart is
    so there must be heaven in us all
We are truly walking angels
    and our destiny does call

We are angels in disguises
    and have believed the roles we played
The curtain call is over
    we can stop the whole charade

We can reveal ourselves as spirit
    and be the angels that we are
To be honest, true and intimate
    is really not bizarre

So if you want to live in heaven
    it is from your heart that you must live
Forgive your past, be good and kind
    it is of your love that you must give.

Relationships

Relationships take many forms
    and never two the same
There are some that lift us to great heights
    and some that bring us shame

But the best relationship of all
    is the one that can't be seen
It is the one that's with yourself
    the most important I would deem

You may find it strange at first
    to say "I love Me" through and through
I tell you it is the greatest gift
    for your world will seem brand new

Now when you have your inner love
    all relationships may change
For you can truly share the best of you
    which at first may seem quite strange

When you amplify your love for self
        your angel wings may sprout
For what it is you have within
        is what you then give out

So cultivate relationships
        that bring you joy and fun
And share the love within yourself
        for you will find that all is one.

Angels, Love and Light

Children

I think there is great wisdom
    in the child's point of view
Adults could learn a thing or two
    to forgive and start anew

Because if a child stumbles
    and ends up in the dirt
They pick themselves right up again
    and do not bother to be hurt

And even for the child
    there is help to get them clean
There are always greater beings
    that assist us when there's need

If we could learn to be as children
    and unlimited in scope
Then we would create our own heaven
    it is for this I have great hope.

The Gift

Out in the woods where it is quiet
        I recline on the earth that is preparing
                for its winter sleep

The autumn air is crisp and cool

The sunlight on my face feels warm and good

There is a gentle breeze
        playing in the tops of the trees

And the nearby lake sparkles
        like diamonds on thick velvet

I have peace in my heart and my mind is calm

My body is relaxed and comfortable
        yet I feel energized
                like a child anticipating a gift

I can sense the nature spirits
>	playing all around

Angels hover near
>	and amplify the good feelings

I enjoy the moment
>	and rest serenely
>	>	in the embrace of nature

As my thoughts turn to gratitude
>	for this gift
>	>	called life.

The Angel of Gold

The angel of gold works night and day
    deep within the earth
He uses light from out the sun
    to form the gold that he gives birth

He reaches up and catches rays
    like ribbons from the sky
Then weaves them through the mountain fast
    like a tapestry on high

These golden threads of love and light
    have greater purpose than you know
For they anchor light into the earth
    that helps us all to grow

Gold has a high vibration
    that is why we like the way it feels
It is precipitated sunshine
    and it helps the earth to heal

The angel of gold is a friend to all
    and the gifts he gives are free
I wish for all to know his love
    and the blessings he decrees.

Sailing Home

Moving forward
    in the face of all
    I cast my fears
        upon the ocean of life

I breeze along
    with the winds of change
    to find smooth sailing
        upon angel wings

My inner compass
    sets the course
    and guides me safely home
        to the truth within my heart.

New World

In this new millennium
I bring the love I have inside
And doubt and fear and hate and greed
are the things I now deny

Our society has toiled
in this grief for far too long
It is time to stop these silly games
that make the ego strong

We have hurt and bound ourselves
in self created chains
And we want to blame the world without
for our self inflicted pain

It is time to take a look within
to forgive and make anew
Take self responsibility
and live honestly and true

The place to start is in the heart
and your feelings deep within
To love yourself and honor self
is the best place to begin

For what we have within ourselves
is what we then give out
And what it is that we give out
will return to us no doubt

I am striving for perfection
of which great masters often speak
It is the light within and the truth therein
and real freedom that I seek

I do my part within my sphere
to maintain harmony
To give up pride and ego
has made me truly free

I know that people really want
a peaceful life of joy
So each must do their quiet part
to share the love that they employ.

About the Author

An ongoing study of the deeper understandings about life has given John T. Goltz a perceptive and loving spirit with a strong desire to assist humanity. He blends his imaginative talent and keen insight with a wealth of natural wisdom. He gladly shares his distinctive awareness and genuine love and is frequently called upon to impart his pragmatic approach to living.

Combining wisdom, experience, and a zest for life, John brings a wonderful, youthful and creative approach to his presentations. His diverse background includes a B.A. in Biology from St. Olaf College - Northfield, MN, various corporate and public relations positions, along with his personal interest in environment and health. He draws upon his broad experience when working with others.

John is the Cofounder and Vice President of the internationally recognized nonprofit, The Love Foundation, and embodies their mission to "inspire people to love unconditionally."

You can reach John through the following web sites:
www.internalinsights.com
www.thelovefoundation.com
www.globalloveday.com
www.whitefirepublishing.com

www.ingramcontent.com/pod-product-compliance
Lightning Source LLC
LaVergne TN
LVHW051703080426
835511LV00017B/2700